Sanjeev Kapoor

Vegetarian

Breakfast Bonanza

In association with Alyona Kapoor

Popular Prakashan
www.popularprakashan.com

Published by
POPULAR PRAKASHAN PVT. LTD.
301, Mahalaxmi Chambers
22, Bhulabhai Desai Road
Mumbai - 400 026
for Khana Khazana Publications Pvt. Ltd.

First Published March 2011
Second Reprint 2014

(4388)
ISBN: 978-81-7991-640-7

Design: Anjali Sawant
Photography: Alim Bolar, Bharat Bhirangi, Mukesh Munim, Sanjeev Nadkarni, Satish Parab and Swapnil Naik

PRINTED IN INDIA
by Saurabh Printers Pvt. Ltd.
A-16, Sector 4, Noida

author's note

Breakfast is the most important meal of the day. Mothers and nutritionists alike have always emphasised the importance of a healthy and hearty breakfast.

However, today, our lives have become increasingly hectic and as a result, our eating habits suffer, and breakfast is the first thing we skip. An inadequate breakfast is as bad as no breakfast, with adverse effects like weight gain due to constant snacking.

In this book you will learn that breakfast doesn't have to be dull and routine. Wake up to an explosion of flavours and discover that breakfast can be delicious, flavourful and nutritious at the same time. No more just chai-biscuit, or plain old cereal on the run.

With my selection of Indian and international vegetarian breakfast dishes, you can look forward to a new breakfast dish every morning of the week. Try the mouth-watering Apple and Cheese Toasts, healthy and light Moong Dal Cheela, exotic Oriental Wraps, and delicious Handvo. Slurp on the filling Banana and Honey Smoothie, or start your day off with peppy Tomato Juice.

With the bonanza of breakfast dishes in this book you can look forward with pleasure to that most important meal of the day!

Happy cooking!

contents

beverages

indian breakfasts

tropical fruit and nut smoothie

1 apple, peeled, cored and sliced

2 ripe mangoes, chopped

2 bananas, sliced

½ cup golden raisins

12-16 pistachios, chopped

Crushed ice, as required

- Place the fruit in a freezer till frozen.
- In a blender, process the frozen fruit, golden raisins and crushed ice, until smooth. Pour into individual tall glasses.
- Serve chilled, decorated with chopped pistachios.

pedewali meethi lassi

4 *malai peda*, grated, to decorate
3 cups yogurt
1 cup sugar
Fresh cream, as required
1 cup ice cubes

- Process the yogurt and sugar for two minutes in a blender. Add the ice cubes and blend for one minute longer.
- Pour into serving glasses. Top with the cream, and decorate with the grated *peda* and serve chilled.

nrg milk shake

4 cups chilled milk
4 *chickoo*, peeled and chopped
8-10 seedless dates, chopped
2 tablespoons sugar
4-5 almonds, blanched, peeled and slivered

- Place the milk, *chickoo*, dates and sugar in a blender and blend till smooth.
- Pour into tall glasses, sprinkle with the almond slivers and serve immediately.

honeyed apple tea

6 tablespoons honey
8 tablespoons apple juice
1 slice of apple, chopped
600 ml brewed black tea
Ice cubes, as required

- Pour the black tea into four tall glasses. Add two tablespoons of apple juice and one and a half tablespoons of honey to each glass and stir to mix well.
- Add the ice cubes and stir. Garnish with the chopped apple and serve chilled.

watermelon smoothie

1 small watermelon, seeded and chopped into small pieces
½ cup strawberry crush
4 sprigs of fresh mint leaves
½ inch ginger, roughly chopped
Ice cubes, as required

- Place the watermelon in a freezer until frozen.
- Process the frozen watermelon in a blender. Add the strawberry crush, mint leaves, ginger and ice cubes, and process again. Serve in individual tall glasses.

melon and orange juice

½ small musk melon, cut into ½-inch cubes

6 oranges

½ medium watermelon, roughly chopped

½ teaspoon *chaat masala*

- Squeeze out the juice from the oranges; strain and set aside. Blend the watermelon pieces in a blender till smooth; strain.
- Mix together the orange juice and watermelon juice. Add the *chaat masala* and mix well. Place in a refrigerator to chill.
- To serve, place one-fourth of the musk melon cubes in each serving glass and pour the blended juice over.
- Serve immediately.

banana and honey smoothie

5 medium bananas, roughly chopped
5 tablespoons honey
2 tablespoons lemon juice
2 cups drained (hung) yogurt
10 fresh mint leaves, torn
10 ice cubes

- Place roughly chopped bananas in a freezer for one hour. Place the frozen banana pieces, honey, lemon juice and yogurt in a blender and blend until smooth.
- Add the ice cubes and blend again. Pour into individual glasses and serve, garnished with mint leaves.

mango smoothie

3 large ripe mangoes, chopped

1 medium ripe mango, cut into ½-inch cubes, to decorate

3 cups chilled milk

6 tablespoons chilled yogurt

8 tablespoons sugar

10-12 ice cubes, crushed

- Place the chopped mangoes in a freezer for a while.
- Blend the chilled mangoes, milk, yogurt, sugar and crushed ice cubes together in a blender.
- Carefully pour the mixture into individual glasses.
- Serve chilled, decorated with mango cubes.

peppy tomato juice

7 ripe red tomatoes, chopped

1½ teaspoons black peppercorns, crushed

2 inches celery stalk, chopped

Salt to taste

1½ tablespoons sugar

Crushed ice, as required

- Sprinkle the salt and the sugar on the tomatoes, and place in a refrigerator for twenty minutes.
- Place the tomatoes and celery along with one and a half cups of water, in a blender, and process till smooth.
- Press the mixture through a strainer and pour into four glasses.
- Serve, sprinkled with the peppercorns and topped with the crushed ice.

chana puri

¾ cup split Bengal gram, soaked overnight

1 inch ginger

2-3 garlic cloves

Salt to taste

1 tablespoon coriander powder

1 tablespoon cumin powder

1 teaspoon red chilli powder

¼ teaspoon turmeric powder

¼ teaspoon dried mango powder

1 tablespoon cumin seeds

½ tablespoon dried pomegranate seeds

1½ tablespoons oil

2 green chillies, slit

1 medium tomato, quartered

½ teaspoon *garam masala* powder

Puri

1 cup wholewheat flour

2 tablespoons semolina

Salt to taste

Oil for deep-frying

- Pound the ginger and garlic to a fine paste.
- Drain the split Bengal gram; add two and half cups of water and salt, and cook till tender. Drain and reserve the cooking liquid.
- Mix together the coriander, cumin, chilli, turmeric and dried mango powders. Dry-roast the cumin seeds and dried pomegranate seeds separately. Cool and grind the seeds together to a powder. Mix together with the rest of the spice powders.
- Heat one tablespoon of oil in a non-stick *kadai.* Add the green chillies and ginger-garlic paste, and stir-fry for a few seconds. Add the mixed spice powder and stir-fry for half a minute. Stir in one-fourth cup of the reserved cooking liquid and cook for two minutes.
- Add the cooked gram, salt, half a cup of the reserved cooking liquid and cook on high heat for three to four minutes, stirring occasionally. Add the tomato and sprinkle *garam masala* powder and roasted pomegranate seed-cumin seed powder.

- Heat the remaining oil and pour over the prepared gram. Stir well and adjust the seasoning.
- For the *puri*, knead the flour and semolina with salt and enough water to make a semi-soft dough. Cover with a damp cloth and rest the dough for half an hour. Divide the dough into twelve equal portions and roll out each portion into a *puri*.
- Heat sufficient oil in a non-stick *kadai* and deep-fry the *puri* on medium heat till golden. Drain on absorbent paper. Serve hot with *chana*.

moong dal cheela

1 cup skinless split green gram, soaked

Salt to taste

¼ teaspoon baking powder

¼ teaspoon turmeric powder

Oil for shallow-frying

Tomato ketchup, as required

Topping

1 large green capsicum, diced

1 small tomato, seeded and diced

1 small onion, diced

4-5 green chillies, chopped (optional)

- Drain the split green gram and grind to a coarse paste. Transfer into a bowl and add salt, baking powder and turmeric powder. Mix well and set aside.
- In a separate bowl, mix together the capsicum, tomato, onion and green chillies. Heat a non-stick *tawa* and pour a small ladleful of the batter and spread it evenly with the back of the ladle in a circular motion, taking care that the pancake is not too thin.
- Drizzle a little oil all around. Spread some of the topping mixture over it. Cook for a minute and turn the *cheela* over. Drizzle a little oil around the edges and cook the other side till golden brown. Serve hot with tomato ketchup.

sabudana vada

1½ cups sago
3 medium potatoes, boiled and mashed
1 cup roasted peanuts, coarsely ground
3 green chillies, finely chopped
2 tablespoons chopped fresh coriander
1 tablespoon lemon juice
Salt to taste
Oil for deep-frying

- Soak the sago in enough water to cover it, for about two hours. Drain the excess water.
- Mix together the sago, potatoes, peanuts, green chillies, chopped coriander, lemon juice and salt. Mix thoroughly.
- Heat the oil in a non-stick *kadai*. Make sixteen lemon-sized balls of the sago mixture, flatten between your palms and deep-fry until golden brown. Serve hot with Coconut Chutney (page 94).

handvo

1 cup rice

½ cup split pigeon peas

¼ cup split green gram

2 tablespoons split Bengal gram

2 tablespoons split black gram

½ cup sour yogurt

2 teaspoons soda bicarbonate

Salt to taste

4 teaspoons sugar

2 teaspoons red chilli powder

½ teaspoon turmeric powder

1 medium carrot, grated

½ cup shelled green peas, boiled

5 tablespoons oil

2 dried red chillies

2 cloves

1 bay leaf

A pinch of asafoetida

2 teaspoons mustard seeds

1 tablespoon lemon juice

3 tablespoons toasted sesame seeds

- Soak the rice with all the gram and pigeon peas in five cups of water for two hours. Drain. Grind the rice mixture to a coarse batter and add enough water to make a batter of medium thick consistency.
- Mix in the yogurt and one teaspoon of soda bicarbonate. Cover the batter and leave to stand in a dark place for two or three hours to ferment. Stir the salt, sugar, chilli powder and turmeric powder into the batter. Mix in the grated carrot and green peas.
- Heat the oil in a non-stick pan; add the red chillies, cloves, bay leaf, asafoetida and mustard seeds, and sauté till the seeds begin to splutter.
- Sprinkle the remaining soda bicarbonate over the batter and pour the lemon juice into it. Immediately pour the hot spices into the batter and whisk briskly.
- Grease a ring mould. Pour the batter into it till half full. Sprinkle the toasted sesame seeds generously over the top. Place about two kilograms of clean sand in a large pressure cooker. Place the ring mould in the sand carefully,

pressing down till it is embedded about half way into the sand. Cover the cooker with the lid but without the gasket and whistle.

- Cook over high heat for ten minutes. Lower heat to medium and cook the handvo till a skewer inserted into it comes out clean. It may take forty to forty-five minutes. Cool slightly and unmould the handvo. Cut into thick slices and serve hot with Green Chutney (page 94).

kanchipuram idli

1 cup short-grained rice

½ cup skinless split black gram

¾ teaspoon fenugreek seeds

1 teaspoon turmeric powder

30 black peppercorns

2 teaspoons split Bengal gram

A pinch of asafoetida

1 cup yogurt

½ cup pure ghee

Salt to taste

A few tender banana leaves

- Soak the rice and black gram with fenugreek seeds for three to four hours.
- Drain and grind to a smooth paste with sufficient water to make a thick batter of pouring consistency. Transfer to a deep bowl.
- Add the turmeric powder, peppercorns, Bengal gram, asafoetida, yogurt, ghee and salt. Mix well and leave to ferment overnight, or for at least six hours.
- Whip the batter well, add one-fourth cup of water to adjust the consistency. The batter should be fairly thick.
- Heat sufficient water in a steamer. Line the *idli* moulds with the banana leaves and pour the batter into them.
- Place in the steamer and steam for about twenty minutes or till risen and fluffy. Serve hot with *sambhar* and Coconut Chutney (page 94).

khaman dhokla

2 cups gram flour

1 cup yogurt, beaten

Salt to taste

1 tablespoon chopped green chillies

1 tablespoon chopped ginger

½ teaspoon turmeric powder

1 teaspoon soda bicarbonate

2 tablespoons oil

Juice of a lemon

1 teaspoon mustard seeds

2 tablespoons chopped green coriander

¼ cup grated fresh coconut

- Place the gram flour in a large bowl. Add the yogurt and one-third cup of warm water. Whisk well, till no lumps remain and the mixture is of a fairly thick consistency. Add salt, mix well and leave to ferment for three to four hours.
- Grind together the green chillies and ginger to a paste.
- Add the chilli-ginger paste, turmeric and salt to the fermented mixture.
- Heat sufficient water in a steamer.
- In a bowl, mix together the soda bicarbonate, one teaspoon of oil and the lemon juice. Add to the fermented mixture.
- Pour the batter into a greased *thali*, and steam for ten to twelve minutes. Set aside to cool. Cut into squares.
- Heat the remaining oil in a small non-stick pan, and add the mustard seeds. When they begin to splutter, pour over the *dhokla*.
- Serve, garnished with chopped coriander and grated coconut.

set dosa

2 cups rice

½ teaspoon fenugreek seeds

1 cup beaten rice

1 cup yogurt

Salt to taste

Oil, as required

- Wash and soak the rice and fenugreek seeds in four cups of warm water for about two hours.
- Soak the beaten rice in a little water for about five minutes. Grind the rice and fenugreek seeds along with the beaten rice into a smooth, thick batter. Add the yogurt and salt, and mix well.
- Leave the batter in a warm place to ferment overnight.
- Heat a non-stick *tawa* and grease it. For each *dosa*, pour a ladleful of batter onto the *tawa*, but do not spread it. The batter will set in a thick round.

- Drizzle a little oil all around the *dosa* and cover it with a lid. Cook till the underside is done and very light brown.
- Serve hot with Coconut Chutney (page 94) or vegetable *kurma*.

Chef's Tip

For added flavour, grind green chillies and ginger with the rest of the ingredients.

rasam vade

Vade

1 cup skinless split black gram, soaked

2-3 tablespoons chopped fresh coconut

2 green chillies, chopped

½ inch ginger, finely chopped

Salt to taste

Oil for deep-frying

Rasam

2 teaspoons *Rasam* Powder (page 95)

2 tablespoons split pigeon peas

2 medium tomatoes, roughly chopped

Salt to taste

1 tablespoon oil

¼ teaspoon asafoetida

½ teaspoon mustard seeds

1-2 dried red chillies, broken into large bits

10-15 curry leaves

1 teaspoon Tamarind Pulp (page 95)

1 teaspoon grated jaggery

1 tablespoon chopped fresh coriander

- Drain the split black gram, and grind to a thick batter. Add the coconut, green chillies, ginger and salt, and whisk well. Heat sufficient oil in a non-stick *kadai*. Divide the mixture into small balls and deep-fry until golden brown. Drain on absorbent paper.
- For the *rasam*, cook the split pigeon peas in one cup of water, until soft. Strain and mash well. Reserve the strained cooking liquid.
- In a deep non-stick pan, place the tomatoes and one cup of water and salt, and cook, till the tomatoes soften. Strain the tomatoes and reserve the stock. Place the strained tomatoes along with the mashed *dal* in a blender and process to a smooth pureé.
- Heat the oil in a non-stick pan; add the asafoetida, mustard seeds, dried chillies and curry leaves. Add the pureé, strained cooking liquid and the tomato stock, *rasam* powder, tamarind pulp, jaggery, chopped coriander and salt. Mix well and simmer, on low heat, for two to three minutes. To serve, place the *vade* in bowls, pour hot *rasam* over and serve immediately.

Chef's Tip

Add a little more *rasam* powder for a spicier *rasam*.

nrg dosa

¼ cup rice flour
¼ cup wheat flour
¼ cup soya flour
¼ cup finger millet flour
Buttermilk, as required
Salt to taste
2 tablespoons chopped fresh coriander
2 green chillies, chopped
Oil for shallow-frying
Tomato ketchup, as required

- Mix together the rice, wheat, soya and millet flour with the buttermilk to make a smooth batter. Add the salt, chopped coriander and green chillies, and mix well. Let the batter rest for about fifteen minutes.
- Heat a thick non-stick *tawa* or frying pan. Add two drops of oil and wipe the *tawa* clean with a piece of wet muslin.
- Add a tablespoon of oil to the *tawa*; pour half a ladleful of batter and spread it to a thin three-inch round. Drizzle a little oil all around. When the underside is cooked, flip the *dosa* and fry the other side. Serve hot with tomato ketchup.

Note: *If you do not have soya flour, you can replace it with gram flour or sorghum flour.*

bombay vegetable sandwich

8 slices white bread
2 medium onions, cut into round slices
1 cucumber, sliced
2 medium tomatoes, cut into round slices
2 medium potatoes, boiled and cut into round slices
2 tablespoons butter + for greasing
½ cup Green Chutney (page 94)
½ teaspoon *chaat masala*
Salt to taste
½ teaspoon crushed peppercorns

- Trim the sides of the bread slices and spread the butter and green chutney on one side of all the bread slices.
- Place four slices of bread on a board, chutney side up, layer it with onion, cucumber, tomato and potato slices. Sprinkle some *chaat masala*, salt and crushed peppercorns. Cover with the remaining slices of bread. Lightly press down so that all the layers are firm and even.
- Place in a lightly buttered sandwich toaster and grill on both sides till brown and crisp. Cut the grilled sandwich with a sharp knife and serve with tomato ketchup and green chutney.

tomato and olive upma

2 medium tomatoes, chopped

10-12 black olives, sliced

1 cup semolina

½ cup yogurt

Salt to taste

3 tablespoons olive oil

½ teaspoon split black gram

¼ teaspoon mustard seeds

5-6 curry leaves

1 large onion, chopped

½ inch ginger, chopped

3-4 green chillies, chopped

2 tablespoons chopped fresh coriander

- Whisk the yogurt with salt and two and a half cups of water to make a very thin buttermilk. Set aside.
- Heat the olive oil in a non-stick *kadai*; add the split black gram and mustard seeds and fry for a minute. When the mustard seeds begin to splutter add the curry leaves, onion, tomatoes, ginger and green chillies, and sauté for a minute.

- Add the semolina and continue to sauté on medium heat for four to five minutes till lightly coloured and fragrant.
- Add the buttermilk, bring to a boil, lower the heat and continue to cook uncovered, stirring continuously, till all the liquid has been absorbed.
- Adjust the seasoning, cover and cook for another two minutes on very low heat.
- Add the black olives and chopped coriander. Stir and cook for a minute. Serve hot.

microwaved kaanda poha

3 medium onions, finely chopped

2 cups thick beaten rice

2 tablespoons oil

3-4 green chillies, slit and seeded

8-10 curry leaves

¼ cup roasted peanuts (optional)

1 teaspoon turmeric powder

Salt to taste

1 tablespoon lemon juice

A few sprigs of fresh coriander, finely chopped

- Wash the beaten rice thoroughly. Drain.
- Place the oil in a microwave-safe bowl along with the onions, green chillies, curry leaves, crushed peanuts. Cook, uncovered, on HIGH (100%) for three minutes.
- Add turmeric powder, beaten rice and salt. Mix well and cook, covered, on HIGH (100%) for five minutes.
- Add lemon juice and mix well. Serve hot, garnished with chopped coriander.

rayalseema pesarettu

1 cup whole green gram

1 medium onion, roughly chopped

1 inch ginger, roughly chopped

4 green chillies, roughly chopped

4 dried red chillies

½ teaspoon black peppercorns, crushed

½ teaspoon cumin seeds, crushed

¼ cup fresh coriander, finely chopped

10-12 curry leaves, finely chopped

1 tablespoon rice flour

Salt to taste

Oil, as required

- Soak the green gram for two to three hours.
- Drain and grind the gram along with the onion, ginger, green and red chillies.
- Add the crushed peppercorns, cumin seeds, chopped coriander; curry leaves, rice flour and salt, and mix well.
- Heat a non-stick *tawa*, and grease it with a little oil.

- Pour a ladleful of batter on the *tawa*, and spread it with the back of the ladle to make a thin six-inch round pancake.
- Pour a little oil around the edges, cover and cook on medium heat, for two to three minutes. Turn over, pour a little oil around the edges and cook the other side for a few minutes until golden brown and crisp.
- Serve hot with Coconut Chutney (page 94) and *sambhar*.

Chef's Tip

Traditionally this dish is very spicy, but you can reduce the amount of chillies, to suit your taste.

kuzhi paniyaram

1 cup rice
1 cup parboiled rice
½ cup skinless split black gram
¼ teaspoon fenugreek seeds
Salt to taste
2 teaspoons oil + for cooking

¼ teaspoon mustard seeds
¼ teaspoon cumin seeds
10-12 curry leaves, chopped
1 large onion, finely chopped
2-3 green chillies, finely chopped

- Soak the rice, parboiled rice, split black gram, and fenugreek seeds in six cups of water for at least five hours.
- Drain and grind to a coarse batter. Add salt, mix well and leave to ferment overnight.
- Heat two teaspoons of oil in a non-stick pan; add the mustard seeds, cumin seeds, curry leaves, onion and green chillies, and sauté for two to three minutes. Add the sizzling spices to the batter and mix well.

- Heat a *paniyaram tawa* on medium heat and grease each mould with a little oil. Pour a ladleful of batter in each mould, drizzle oil and cook for four to five minutes till the underside is done.
- Turn them over using a spoon and drizzle a little more oil and continue to cook for three to four minutes, or until both the sides are evenly cooked. Serve hot with Coconut Chutney (page 94).

Note: *A paniyaram tawa is a tawa with several round moulds in it. It is also used to make appe.*

onion and capsicum uttappam

2 cups rice, soaked

1 cup skinless split black gram, soaked

Salt to taste

Topping

2 medium onions, finely chopped

2 medium green capsicums, finely chopped

- Drain and grind the rice and split black gram separately, using very little water, to a smooth batter.
- In a large bowl, mix together both the batters. Cover and leave to ferment for six to eight hours, in a warm place.
- Place the fermented batter in a bowl, add salt and sufficient water to get the desired consistency and mix well.
- Heat a non-stick *tawa* and pour a small ladleful of the batter and spread it evenly with the back of the ladle in a circular motion, taking care that it is not too thin.

- Sprinkle onion and capsicum and a little water all around. Cover and cook, on medium heat, until the underside is done.
- Flip it over and sprinkle a little water around. Cover and cook till the other side is done too.
- Serve hot with tomato chutney.

seyal dabal

1 loaf of sliced bread

4 tablespoons oil

A pinch of asafoetida

½ teaspoon cumin seeds

¼ teaspoon mustard seeds

1 medium onion, chopped

2 medium tomatoes, chopped

2 green chillies, chopped

¼ teaspoon turmeric powder

2 teaspoons coriander powder

1 teaspoon red chilli powder

Salt to taste

2 tablespoons chopped fresh coriander

1 teaspoon lemon juice

- Trim the edges of the bread slices if you wish. Tear them into medium pieces.
- Heat the oil in a non-stick pan; add the asafoetida, cumin seeds, mustard seeds and onion, and sauté till the onions turn translucent.
- Add the tomatoes and stir. Add the green chillies, turmeric powder, coriander powder and chilli powder, and sauté for two to three minutes.
- Add one cup of water and salt to taste. When the water comes to a boil add the bread and mix well.
- When all the water has been absorbed, sprinkle the chopped coriander and mix lightly. Add the lemon juice and mix.
- Serve at once.

aloo anardana kulcha

2 medium potatoes, boiled and grated

1 teaspoon dried pomegranate seeds, roasted and coarsely powdered

2 cups refined flour

¼ teaspoon soda bicarbonate

Salt to taste

2 tablespoons yogurt

2 tablespoons milk

4 tablespoons olive oil

½ medium onion, chopped

¼ cup chopped fresh coriander

8-10 fresh mint leaves, chopped

2 green chillies, chopped

½ tablespoon red chilli powder

1 tablespoon roasted cumin powder

¾ teaspoon onion seeds

2 tablespoons extra-virgin olive oil

- Sift the refined flour with the soda bicarbonate and salt into a bowl. Gradually mix in the yogurt and milk. Add sufficient water to make a soft, smooth dough. Cover with a damp cloth and rest the dough for ten minutes.
- Add two tablespoons of olive oil and knead the dough well. Cover it once again and set aside for at least an hour.

- Divide the dough into six to eight equal portions and shape them into smooth balls.
- Preheat an oven to 220°C/425°F/Gas Mark 7. Grease a baking tray with a little olive oil.
- Mix together the potatoes, onion, chopped coriander, mint leaves, green chillies, dried pomegranate seed powder, chilli powder, roasted cumin powder and salt to taste. Divide the potato mixture into six to eight equal portions and set aside. Flatten a portion of dough, place a portion of the potato mixture in the centre and fold the edges over to form a ball.
- Place each stuffed ball on a lightly floured surface and roll gently into a four to five-inch round. Brush lightly with a little of the remaining olive oil, sprinkle a few onion seeds on the surface and press lightly with your palm.
- Place the *kulcha* on the greased baking tray and bake in the preheated oven for about six to eight minutes. Brush the hot *kulcha* with extra-virgin olive oil and serve immediately.

bhajnee thalipeeth

3 cups *bhajnee* flour (recipe below)

Salt to taste

½ teaspoon turmeric powder

1 medium onion, chopped

7 tablespoons oil

- Place *bhajnee* flour in a bowl with the salt, turmeric powder, chopped onion and two teaspoons of oil. Add water, a little at a time, and make a soft dough.
- Divide the dough into eight equal portions. Flatten each portion into a quarter-inch thick, four to five-inch round on a dampened banana leaf, or thick polythene sheet.
- Make a hole in the centre of each *thalipeeth*. Heat a non-stick *tawa*, and spread a little oil over it. Transfer *thalipeeth* carefully onto the *tawa*. Spoon a little oil around the sides and cook on low heat for one minute.

4. Turn the *thalipeeth* and cook the other side for one minute, or till crisp and golden brown. Serve hot with a dollop of butter or yogurt.

bhajnee flour

1 cup wholewheat flour

1 cup rice

2 cups sorghum

2 cups millet

¾ cup split Bengal gram

¾ cup skinless split black gram

½ cup coriander seeds

- Dry-roast each ingredient separately. Cool, mix and grind to a fine powder. *Bhajnee* flour can be stored for up to one month.

aloo gobhi parantha

3 medium potatoes, boiled and mashed

½ medium cauliflower, grated

3 cups wholewheat flour + for dusting

Salt to taste

2 tablespoons oil + for shallow-frying

2 tablespoons chopped fresh coriander

3 green chillies, crushed

½ inch ginger, grated

½ teaspoon red chilli powder

- Place the flour in a deep bowl. Add the salt to taste and rub in two tablespoons of oil. Add water and knead well to make a stiff dough. Cover and rest the dough for fifteen to twenty minutes.
- Mix together the potatoes and cauliflower. Add the chopped coriander, green chillies, ginger, chilli powder and salt to taste, and mix again.
- Divide the dough into eight equal portions and shape them into small *pede* (flattened balls). Cover with a damp cloth and rest the dough again for five minutes.

- Flatten each *peda* by pressing it with your fingers so that the edges are thinner than the centre. Place one portion of potato-cauliflower mixture in the centre of the flattened dough, gather the edges together and shape again into a *peda*. Seal the edges completely so that the stuffing does not ooze out.
- Sprinkle a little flour on a smooth surface. Flatten each stuffed *peda* again, and roll out into a six-inch round *parantha*.
- Heat a non-stick *tawa*; place each *parantha* on it and cook on moderate heat for two minutes on either side. Spread half a tablespoon of oil on one side of the *parantha*, flip over and spread half a tablespoon of oil on the other side as well. Cook over low heat till both sides are golden brown.
- Serve hot with fresh yogurt or mango pickle.

bikaneri dal paranthe

1¼ cups split Bengal gram, soaked

1½ cups refined flour + for dusting

Salt to taste

6 tablespoons pure ghee

¼ teaspoon asafoetida

1 teaspoon coriander powder

1 teaspoon red chilli powder

½ teaspoon *garam masala* powder

Oil for shallow-frying

- Combine the refined flour, salt and four tablespoons of ghee. Add sufficient water and knead to make a soft, smooth dough. Cover with a damp cloth and rest the dough for ten minutes.
- Pressure-cook the split Bengal gram with two cups of water and salt till the pressure is released two or three times (two or three whistles).
- Remove the lid when the pressure reduces and set the gram aside to cool. Grind to a coarse paste.
- Heat the remaining ghee in a non-stick *kadai*.
- Add the asafoetida, coriander powder, chilli powder and *garam masala* powder. Sauté for half a minute.
- Add the ground gram and cook for three to four minutes or till dry. Adjust the seasoning and mix well.
- Remove from heat and set aside to cool. Divide into eight equal portions and set aside.

- Divide the dough into eight equal portions and roll into balls.
- Shape each portion of dough on your palm into a small *puri*; place a portion of the stuffing in the centre, gather up the edges and shape into a ball again.
- Press each ball down lightly on the tabletop. Roll out into a thin *parantha*, dusting with flour if required. The *parantha* should be as thin as a papad.
- Heat sufficient oil in a pan. Slide a *parantha* gently into the oil and shallow-fry till evenly golden brown on both sides.
- Drain on absorbent paper and serve hot.

methi khakhra

1 teaspoon dried fenugreek leaves

2 cups wholewheat flour

Salt to taste

¼ teaspoon tumeric powder

1 teaspoon cumin powder

1 teaspoon ginger-green chilli paste

- Mix together the flour and the salt in a bowl. Add the turmeric powder, cumin powder, ginger-green chilli paste and dried fenugreek leaves, and mix well. Add enough water and knead into a medium soft dough.
- Divide the dough into twelve equal balls. Roll out each ball into a very thin, round *chapati*.
- Heat a non-stick *tawa*; place a *chapati* on it and roast on low heat. Turn over and press the *chapati* with a wooden press. Continue pressing and turning till the *khakra* is evenly cooked on both sides.
- The *khakra* is done when it is light brown and crisp. Remove from heat, allow to cool and store in an airtight container, handling it carefully as it is crisp and may break.

thepla

2 cups wholewheat flour

½ cup gram flour

1 cup chopped fresh fenugreek

¼ teaspoon turmeric powder

½ teaspoon red chilli powder

1 teaspoon ginger-green chilli paste

2 tablespoons olive oil + for shallow-frying

Salt to taste

Yogurt, as required

- Place the wholewheat flour, gram flour, chopped fenugreek, turmeric powder, chilli powder, ginger-green chilli paste, two tablespoons olive oil and salt in a bowl and mix well.
- Add sufficient yogurt and knead into a semi-soft dough. Cover with a damp cloth and set aside for fifteen minutes.
- Divide the dough into sixteen equal balls and roll out into thin *thepla*.
- Heat a non-stick *tawa* and roast the *thepla*, applying a little oil on either side, till both the sides are evenly golden brown. *Thepla* can be eaten hot or cold.

mooli ke paranthe

3 medium radishes with leaves

3 cups wholewheat flour + for dusting

Salt to taste

2 tablespoons ghee + for shallow-frying

½ teaspoon red chilli powder

¼ teaspoon carom seeds, crushed

2 green chillies, chopped

2 tablespoons chopped fresh coriander

- Grate the radish and finely chop the radish leaves. Squeeze out the juice from the grated radish. Reserve the radish and the juice separately.
- Mix together the wholewheat flour and salt in a bowl. Rub in two tablespoons of ghee with your fingertips. Add the reserved radish juice and knead into a soft dough, adding a little water if necessary. Cover with a damp cloth and rest the dough for fifteen minutes.

- Combine the grated radish, chopped leaves, chilli powder, carom seeds, green chillies and chopped coriander in a bowl. Divide the mixture into eight equal portions.
- Divide the dough into eight equal portions. Flatten each portion, making the edges thinner than the centre. Place a portion of the filling in the centre and sprinkle with salt. Gather the edges together and roll into a ball.
- Press the ball slightly to flatten, and roll out into a *parantha* on a greased and floured board or table.
- Heat a non-stick *tawa*. Place a *parantha* on the non-stick *tawa* and cook for one minute. Turn over and drizzle a little ghee over it. Turn over once again and drizzle a little ghee on the other side. Cook till both sides are golden and crisp on the outside.
- Serve hot.

teekhat meethachi puri

2 teaspoons red chilli powder

Salt to taste

1 cup wholewheat flour

3 tablespoons semolina

½ teaspoon turmeric powder

1 teaspoon carom seeds

2 tablespoons oil + for deep-frying

- Sift together the wholewheat flour and salt.
- Add the semolina, chilli powder, turmeric powder, carom seeds and two tablespoons of oil, and mix well. Add water, a little at a time and knead into a medium hard dough. Cover with a damp cloth for half an hour.
- Divide the dough into twelve to sixteen equal portions. Shape each portion into a ball and roll out into a three to four-inch *puri*.
- Heat the oil in a non-stick *kadai* and deep-fry the *puri* on both sides till puffed up and light golden brown. Drain on absorbent paper. Serve immediately.

Chef's Tip

These *puri* can be eaten as an evening snack with pickle, or served as an accompaniment to a main course.

patoli

1½ cups rice

A pinch of salt

Oil, as required

Pure ghee, as required

8 turmeric leaves

Stuffing

1 cup grated coconut

6 tablespoons grated jaggery

¼ teaspoon green cardamom powder

- Soak the rice in four cups of water for two hours. Drain and grind into a thick paste using very little water. Add salt to taste, cover and rest the batter for an hour.
- For the stuffing, cook the grated coconut, jaggery, and cardamom powder, in a non-stick pan on low heat, till all the moisture dries up.
- Lightly grease the turmeric leaves on the shiny side with oil. Spread a little of the prepared rice batter on the greased side. Spread the stuffing on one side of the leaf and fold the other side of the leaf over.
- Arrange the *patoli* in a colander and cook in a steamer for ten to fifteen minutes. Serve hot, drizzled with pure ghee.

sweet pongal

1½ cups rice
½ cup skinless split green gram
4 green cardamoms
1 tablespoon sugar
2 cups crumbled jaggery
2½ cups milk
½ cup pure ghee
½ cup grated coconut
¼ teaspoon grated nutmeg
4 tablespoons raisins
12-15 cashew nuts
A pinch of edible camphor (optional)

- Soak the rice for half an hour. Drain and set aside.
- Lightly dry-roast the split green gram in a hot non-stick *kadai*.
- Grind the cardamoms with sugar to a fine powder. Sift and set aside.
- Boil milk with one cup of water in a thick-bottomed non-stick pan.
- Add the rice and the green gram to the boiling milk. Bring the milk to a boil again, stirring continuously. Lower the heat and simmer for fifteen

minutes, stirring occasionally, until the rice and *dal* are completely cooked. You can also pressure-cook the mixture.

- Add the jaggery and stir continuously to prevent the mixture from sticking to the bottom of the pan. Cook until the jaggery melts completely. Add half the ghee and continue cooking, over low heat, for about five minutes, stirring frequently.
- Heat the remaining ghee in a separate non-stick pan and lightly fry the grated coconut. Add the grated nutmeg, raisins and cashew nuts, and stir well. Add the fried mixture to the cooked *pongal*.
- Sprinkle the cardamom and the camphor powder over the *pongal*, stir well and serve hot.

Chef's Tip

You can use sugar or palm jaggery instead of regular jaggery.
Add coconut milk instead of grated coconut for a richer taste.

coconut sheera

2 tablespoons grated coconut

½ cup chopped tender coconut flesh, for decorating

1 cup semolina

3 tablespoons ghee

2 cups milk

¼ cup *khoya/mawa*, crumbled

9 tablespoons sugar

- Heat two tablespoons of ghee in a non-stick pan. Add the semolina and fry till fragrant. Add the grated coconut and continue to fry.
- Add the milk, *mawa*, and sugar, and mix well. Cook till the semolina is cooked and the mixture resembles *halwa*. Add the remaining ghee to give it a glaze.
- Pack the *sheera* into small moulds, and unmould onto serving plates.
- Decorate with the tender coconut and serve.

jalebi

1½ cups refined flour

1 teaspoon soda bicarbonate

A pinch of yellow or saffron food colour (optional)

2½ cups sugar

½ teaspoon cardamom powder

Ghee for deep-frying

- Mix together the flour and soda bicarbonate. Add some water and stir well to make a smooth batter. Add the yellow or saffron food colour and mix well. Set aside to ferment overnight, or for at least six hours.
- Stir, adding a little water if required, to make a batter of pouring consistency.
- Make a sugar syrup by cooking equal quantities of sugar and water with the cardamom powder for twenty minutes.
- Heat the ghee in a *jalebi tawi*, or a non-stick *kadai*.

- Pour the batter into a *jalebi* cloth. Squeeze the batter through the hole in a *jalebi* design into the moderately hot ghee. Start piping from the outside to the inside for better results.
- Cook the *jalebi* on both sides till crisp. Soak *jalebi* in sugar syrup for at least five minutes before serving.

Chef's Tip

For the *jalebi* cloth, make a 3mm hole in the centre of a piece of cloth. *Jalebi* making takes some practice and patience. To start with, try making individual *jalebi* and when you have perfected that, try making them together in a row. To make crisp *jalebi* add a little rice flour to the refined flour.

corn and bean burritos

100 grams sweetcorn kernels
250 grams sprouted beans, blanched
4 refined flour tortillas
½ cup grated mozzarella cheese
Salt to taste
10-12 black peppercorns, crushed
1 tablespoon lemon juice
1 medium tomato, chopped
½ cup shredded lettuce
2 spring onions, chopped
2 green chillies, chopped
½ cup Salsa (page 95)
Chilled sour cream, to serve

- Preheat an oven to 200°C/400°F/Gas Mark 6.
- Mix together the cheese, salt, crushed peppercorns, lemon juice and sprouted beans in a bowl.
- In another bowl, mix together the tomato, lettuce and spring onions. Add the corn and green chillies, and mix.

- Place the tortillas on a plate. Layer equal portions of the cheese and bean mixture and the corn and tomato mixture on each tortilla. Sprinkle the salsa on top and fold each tortilla over.
- Arrange the tortillas in a baking dish and bake for twenty minutes.
- Serve hot with the chilled sour cream.

pancake triangles

⅓ cup refined flour

⅓ cup wholewheat flour

1 teaspoon baking powder

Salt to taste

1½ cups milk

4 teaspoons oil

Filling

1 teaspoon butter

2 spring onions, chopped

2 green capsicums, chopped

¾ cup sweetcorn kernels, cooked

Salt to taste

¼ teaspoon black pepper powder

¼ teaspoon mustard paste

1 tablespoon tomato ketchup

- For the pancakes, sift the flours with the baking powder and salt into a deep bowl. Add the milk and whisk well to prevent lumps from forming. Let the batter rest for ten minutes.

- For the filling, heat the butter in a non-stick pan. Add the spring onions and sauté for one minute.
- Add the capsicums, corn, salt, pepper powder and mustard paste, and sauté for one minute. Remove from heat and stir in the tomato ketchup. Set aside.
- For each pancake, heat one teaspoon of oil in a six-inch non-stick frying pan.
- Pour a ladleful of the batter and swirl the pan so that the batter spreads evenly around. Cook till the underside is lightly browned. Cook only on one side and remove.
- Place each pancake, with the cooked side down, on a flat surface and cut in half. Spoon a portion of the stuffing on one side of each half and fold over the other side to make a triangle.
- Press the edges down well and serve immediately.

apple and cheese toasts

2 large apples, cored and cut into thick slices

120 grams cottage cheese, grated

4 wholewheat bread slices

3 teaspoons lemon juice

½ cup orange juice

8 cashew nuts, toasted and coarsely crushed

½ teaspoon cinnamon powder

1 tablespoon honey

- Preheat an oven to 180°C/350°F/Gas Mark 4. Sprinkle one teaspoon of lemon juice on the apple slices.
- Heat a non-stick pan and gently poach the apple slices in the orange and remaining lemon juice for about ten minutes or until soft, turning them over carefully to cook evenly.
- Toast the bread slices and trim the sides.
- Mix together the cottage cheese and crushed cashew nuts. Spread the mixture on the toasted bread and arrange the cooked apple slices on top.

- Sprinkle the cinnamon powder and place the toasts in the preheated oven or under a hot grill until light golden.
- Drizzle the honey on the hot toasts, cut into desired shapes and serve.

corn panzza

4 four-inch wholewheat pizza breads

2 tablespoons olive oil

Tomato Sauce

2 medium tomatoes, puréed

4 tablespoons tomato ketchup

1 tablespoon olive oil

2 garlic cloves, chopped

1 small onion, chopped

Salt to taste

½ teaspoon sugar

6-8 black peppercorns, crushed

1 teaspoon oregano

Topping

1½ cups blanched American corn kernels

4-5 black peppercorns, crushed

2 cups grated mozzarella cheese

- For the tomato sauce, heat the oil in a non-stick pan; add the garlic and sauté for half a minute. Add the onion and sauté till translucent.
- Stir in the tomato purée and cook till thick. Add the tomato ketchup and cook for another five to eight minutes.

- Add the salt, sugar, crushed peppercorns and oregano, and mix well. Set aside to cool.
- Heat half a tablespoon of olive oil in a non-stick pan and place a pizza base on it. Spread a quarter of the tomato sauce evenly on the pizza. Scatter one-fourth of the corn over the sauce and sprinkle the crushed peppercorns. Top with one-fourth of the grated cheese.
- Cover the pan with a lid and cook on very low heat for ten minutes, or till the base has evenly browned and the cheese has melted. Cut into wedges and serve hot.

Chef's Tip

For younger children you can serve half a pizza per child or use baby pizza breads.

oriental wraps

2 pita breads

1 cup bean curd (tofu) cubes

Chilli-garlic sauce, as required

½ cup shredded carrot

½ cup shredded red cabbage

2 spring onions with greens, sliced

Sesame Dressing

2 tablespoon roasted sesame seeds

¼ inch ginger

1 garlic clove

1 tablespoon soy sauce

2 tablespoons rice wine vinegar

2 teaspoons sugar

Salt to taste

- For the dressing, powder the sesame seeds in a blender. Add the ginger and garlic and blend for half a minute. Add the soy sauce, rice wine vinegar, sugar and salt, and blend some more. If the mixture is too thick, add a little water. Transfer the dressing to a bowl.
- Preheat an oven to 200^{0}C/400^{0}F/Gas Mark 6.
- Marinate the bean curd in two tablespoons of sesame dressing for fifteen minutes.
- Place the bean curd on a baking sheet and bake for thirty minutes. Reserve the remaining marinade. Take the bean curd out of the oven and set aside to cool.
- Spread the chilli-garlic sauce on each pita bread. Place a layer each of red cabbage, carrots and spring onions with greens on top. Arrange the baked tofu over the vegetables.
- Drizzle the remaining marinade over the bean curd. Roll up and cut each pita bread into half. Serve immediately.

vegetable club sandwiches

1 medium carrot, grated

1 medium capsicum, cut into thin strips

¼ medium cabbage, grated

½ medium head of lettuce

2 medium tomatoes, sliced

1 medium cucumber, sliced

12 slices white bread

¼ cup Eggless Mayonnaise (page 94)

2 pineapple slices, cut into small pieces

Salt to taste

¼ teaspoon white pepper powder

4 tablespoons butter

4 cheese slices

- Toast the bread slices.
- To make the coleslaw, mix together the mayonnaise, carrot, capsicum and cabbage. Add the pineapple and season with salt and pepper. Set aside some of the coleslaw to serve as an accompaniment to the sandwich.

- Spread the butter on one side of all the toasted bread slices, and on both sides of four slices. Place four single side buttered bread slices, on a board. Place half the lettuce leaves on the slices and spread the remaining coleslaw evenly on all four slices. Arrange another layer of bread slices, with both sides buttered, on top. Place the remaining lettuce leaves, tomato and cucumber slices on top and sprinkle some salt and pepper. Place the cheese slices on top of the vegetables.
- Cover with the final layer of toasted bread slices. Lightly press down with your palm.
- Using a very sharp knife cut the edges of each sandwich. Cut the sandwiches diagonally to make triangles. Serve with the reserved coleslaw and potato wafers.

Chef's Tip

You can add a tomato omelette in between the layers as well.

garden wraps

4 refined flour tortillas

½ cup cream cheese

1 cup shredded iceberg lettuce

1 medium onion, sliced

2 medium cucumbers, cut into thin strips

2 medium tomatoes, cut into thin strips

½ cup bean sprouts

1 teaspoon red chilli flakes

Salt to taste

- Spread the cream cheese on the tortillas.
- Top with the lettuce, onion, cucumbers, tomatoes and bean sprouts. Sprinkle the chilli flakes and salt on top.
- Roll up each tortilla tightly. Cut in half and serve immediately.

herb and onion bread

1½ teaspoons mixed dried herbs

2 medium onions, minced or grated

560 grams wholewheat flour

20 grams fresh yeast

1 teaspoon sugar

1⅛ cup warm water

½ cup milk

60 grams butter

1½ teaspoons salt

- Crumble yeast into a cup and sprinkle with the sugar. Add two tablespoons of warm water and mix until smooth.
- Set in a warm place for ten minutes, or until the mixture becomes frothy.
- Pour the milk into a pan and heat gently. Remove from heat just before the milk begins to boil.
- Chop the butter, drop into the milk and add the remaining warm water.
- Set aside for ten minutes, or until the butter has completely melted and the milk remains lukewarm.

- Put the flour and salt into a large bowl. Add the herbs and the onion, and mix thoroughly. Make a well in the centre; add the yeast mixture and the lukewarm milk-butter mixture. Mix lightly to make a soft dough.
- Cover with a damp cloth and leave in a warm place for two hours, or until the dough has doubled in size. Oil two four-hundred-and-fifty grams loaf tins. Knead the dough once again well and divide into two.
- Shape the dough into loaves and put it into the tins. Cover and leave to rise for forty-five minutes, or until the dough is almost double in size.
- Preheat an oven to 180^{0}C/350^{0}F/Gas Mark 4. Place the loaves in the oven and bake for forty-five minutes. Increase the heat to 220^{0}C/425^{0}F/Gas Mark 7 and bake for another twenty minutes.
- Remove from the tins and cool on a wire rack. Slice and serve fresh and warm.

Chef's Tip

Use fresh herbs for a better flavour.

bread rolls

3¾ cups refined flour
15 grams fresh yeast
2 teaspoons sugar
1½ teaspoons salt
30 grams butter

- Combine the yeast with sugar and one-fourth cup lukewarm water, stir and set aside for ten to fifteen minutes to froth.
- Sift the flour and salt together into a bowl. Add the yeast mixture and knead, adding water a little at a time, till you use up one cup of water.
- Stretch and knead till you get a smooth, elastic dough. Cover with a damp cloth and set aside till it doubles in size.
- Knock back the dough and divide into twenty equal portions. Shape into smooth round balls and then into any shape of your choice.

- Place the rolls on a greased baking tray, cover with a damp cloth and set aside for fifteen minutes or till they double in size again.
- Preheat an oven 190°C/375°F/Gas Mark 5.
- Place the baking tray in the oven and bake for twenty-five to thirty minutes till golden brown and soft to the touch.
- Remove from the oven, brush with melted butter and transfer to a wire rack to cool.

chilli-cheese toast

4-6 green chillies, finely chopped

1½ cups grated cheese

8 slices bread

150 grams fresh coriander, chopped

1 medium onion, chopped

1 medium capsicum, chopped (optional)

1 teaspoon black peppercorns, crushed

Salt to taste

- Preheat an oven to 180°C/350°F/Gas Mark 4.
- In a bowl, mix together the green chillies, cheese, chopped coriander, onion, capsicum, crushed peppercorns and salt. Divide the mixture into eight equal portions.
- Toast the bread slices on one side on a non-stick *tawa*. Apply the cheese mixture on the non-toasted side of the bread slices.
- Cook in the preheated oven or place under a hot grill until the cheese melts and turns golden brown. Cut each slice diagonally into two and serve hot with tomato sauce.

spiced wholemeal and oat pancakes

1 cup wholewheat flour

¼ cup porridge oats

2 tablespoons powdered sugar

¼ teaspoon baking powder

¼ teaspoon soda bicarbonate

½ teaspoon cinnamon powder

1½ cups buttermilk

Maple syrup or honey, as required

- Place the wholewheat flour in a bowl and add the oats and powdered sugar, and mix well. Add the baking powder, soda bicarbonate, cinnamon powder, and mix.
- Gradually add the buttermilk, whisking continuously, to make a moderately thick, smooth batter.
- Heat a non-stick pan. Pour a ladleful of batter and swirl to spread the batter around the pan. Cook, on low heat, till the underside is done.
- Flip the pancake over and cook the other side.
- Serve hot with maple syrup or honey.

wheat biscuits

1¼ cups wholewheat flour

2 tablespoons wheat bran

⅓ cup refined flour

110 grams chilled butter, diced

½ cup powdered sugar

⅓ cup milk

- Preheat the oven to 170°C/325°F/Gas Mark 3.
- In a bowl, mix together the wholewheat flour, bran and refined flour. Add the diced butter and rub it in with your fingertips till the mixture resembles breadcrumbs.
- Mix in the powdered sugar. Add the cold milk (or water, or a mixture of the two) and knead lightly making sure you do not overwork the dough.
- Sprinkle some flour on the worktop and roll out the dough into a one-fourth inch thick rectangle. Cut out biscuits with cookie cutters of assorted shapes. Place the biscuits a little apart on a baking tray. Bake for twenty to twenty-five minutes, or till golden brown.
- Remove from the oven and transfer the cookies to a wire rack to cool. Store in an airtight tin.

oats with dried fruit in milk

1½ cups oats

8-10 almonds, slivered

¼ cup dried apricots, chopped

⅓ cup prunes, chopped

6 cups milk

4 tablespoons sugar

- Roast the oats in a non-stick pan for two minutes. Add the milk and bring to a boil.
- Add the almonds and cook for ten minutes, until thick.
- Add the sugar and stir to dissolve. Add the apricots and prunes, and mix.
- Serve hot.

banana yogurt custard

2 large ripe bananas, grated

4 tablespoons drained (hung) yogurt, whisked

3 tablespoons vanilla custard powder

2 cups milk

4 tablespoons sugar

4 tablespoons grated chocolate

- Place the custard powder in a non-stick pan. Add milk and mix well. Cook on medium heat, stirring continuously till thickened. Cool.
- Add sugar to the custard and mix.
- Place the bananas in a large bowl. Add the drained yogurt and the cooled custard, and mix.
- Transfer the mixture into serving bowls. Decorate with the grated chocolate and serve.

- **coconut chutney**

Grind 1 cup grated fresh coconut (white portion only), with very little water into a thick chutney. Add salt. Sauté 2 broken dried red chillies, ¼ teaspoon mustard seeds and ½ teaspoon skinless split black gram in 2 tablespoons of oil. Add a large pinch of asafoetida and 7-8 curry leaves. Pour over the chutney and cover for a while. Mix thoroughly. Variation: add ginger or garlic.

- **eggless mayonnaise**

Whisk together ¼ cup cream, ¼ teaspoon mustard paste, ½ teaspoon lemon juice, ½ teaspoon black pepper powder and salt to taste in a clean dry bowl. Add ¾ cup oil a little by little, whisking continuously, till all the oil is incorporated.

- **green chutney**

Grind together 1 cup fresh coriander, ½ cup fresh mint, 2-3 green chillies, black salt to taste, ¼ teaspoon sugar and 1 tablespoon lemon juice to a smooth paste using a little water if required.

- **rasam powder**

Heat ½ tablespoon of olive oil in a *kadai* and sauté 1 teaspoon asafoetida and 20 curry leaves for half a minute. Roast separately 15 whole dried red chillies, 1 tablespoon cumin seeds, 2 tablespoons coriander seeds, 1 teaspoon fenugreek seeds, 1 tablespoon roasted split Bengal gram. Cool, mix and grind along with asafoetida and curry leaves to a fine powder.Cool and store in an airtight container.

- **salsa**

Roast 2 halved large onions, 5 halved garlic cloves, 4 halved medium tomatoes and 1 quartered capsicum on a hot griddle till the skins are charred. Cool and grind coarsely with salt. Transfer to a bowl and stir in the lemon juice.

- **tamarind pulp**

Soak 75 grams tamarind in 100 ml warm water for 10-15 minutes. Grind to a smooth paste and strain to remove any fibres. Store in an airtight container in the refrigerator.

glossary

English	Hindi	English	Hindi
Asafoetida	Hing	Parboiled rice	Ukda chawal
Bean sprouts	Ankurit moong	Prunes	Sookhe adu
Beaten rice	Poha	Radish	Mooli
Cinnamon	Dalchini	Refined flour	Maida
Cloves	Laung	Sago	Sabudana
Coriander seeds	Dhania	Semolina	Sooji/rawa
Cumin seeds	Jeera	Sesame seeds	Til
Dried fenugreek leaves	Kasoori methi	Skinless split black gram	Dhuli urad dal
Dried mango powder	Aamchur	Skinless split green gram	Dhuli moong dal
Dried pomegranate kernels	Anardana	Sorghum	Jowar
Fenugreek seeds	Methi dana	Split Bengal gram	Chana dal
Gram flour	Besan	Split pigeon peas	Toovar dal/arhar dal
Green cardamoms	Chhoti elaichi	Spring onion greens	Hare pyaaz ke patte
Jaggery	Gur	Spring onions	Hare pyaaz
Millet	Bajra	Tamarind	Imli
Musk melon	Kharbooj	Watermelon	Tarbooj
Nutmeg	Jaiphal	Whole green gram	Sabut moong dal
Oats	Jaee	Wholewheat flour	Atta
Olives	Jaitun	Whreat bran	Gehun ka Chokar
Onion seeds	Kalonji	Yogurt	Dahi